PRINCEWILL LAGANG

The Pursuit of Purity: A Christian Guide to Dating

First published by PRINCEWILL LAGANG 2023

Copyright © 2023 by Princewill Lagang

All rights reserved. No part of this publication may be reproduced, stored or transmitted in any form or by any means, electronic, mechanical, photocopying, recording, scanning, or otherwise without written permission from the publisher. It is illegal to copy this book, post it to a website, or distribute it by any other means without permission.

Princewill Lagang asserts the moral right to be identified as the author of this work.

First edition

This book was professionally typeset on Reedsy.
Find out more at reedsy.com

Contents

1	The Foundation of Love	1
2	Self-Awareness and Motivation	4
3	Aligning Values in Christian Dating	7
4	Setting Healthy Boundaries	10
5	The Role of Family and Friends in Your Christian Dating...	13
6	Seeking God's Guidance Through Prayer	16
7	Embracing Patience and Trusting God's Timing	19
8	A Recap of Christian Dating Principles	22
9	Navigating Challenges and Preserving Purity	25
10	Celebrating Your Love Story	28
11	Nurturing a Lasting, God-Honoring Relationship	31
12	Passing on the Legacy of Purity	34

1

The Foundation of Love

A gentle breeze rustled through the trees on a warm Sunday afternoon. Birds chirped harmoniously, providing the soundtrack for an idyllic church picnic. In the midst of the laughter and chatter, Sarah sat on a checkered blanket, her eyes fixed on the horizon. She had been a dedicated member of her church for years, and as a young woman, her thoughts often wandered to the topic of dating.

The pursuit of purity in dating was a topic that had been on her mind for some time. Like many Christians, she sought a deeper understanding of how her faith could guide her in forming meaningful and God-honoring relationships. As the sun's rays caressed her face, she began to reflect on the journey she was about to embark upon.

The Yearning for Love

Dating is not merely a secular concept; it is a universal human experience. The yearning for love, companionship, and connection is woven into the fabric of our existence. From the very beginning, when God created Adam and Eve, he declared, "It is not good for man to be alone" (Genesis 2:18, NIV).

In those simple words, God acknowledged the profound need for human connection. Yet, the Bible offers more than just recognition of this need; it provides guidance on how to pursue love in a way that aligns with God's plan.

The Purpose of Dating

For Christians, dating isn't just about finding a life partner or satisfying emotional needs; it's a sacred journey with a higher purpose. In this pursuit, the principles of purity and love go hand in hand. Purity in dating is about maintaining a heart and mind focused on God's plan, honoring both yourself and your potential partner, and seeking a relationship that glorifies Him. Purity, in this context, is not limited to physical boundaries but extends to the emotional, spiritual, and mental aspects of the relationship.

The Roadmap Ahead

As Sarah contemplated her future, she realized that the path toward purity in dating was both exciting and challenging. She knew that it would require introspection, a deep understanding of her faith, and a commitment to honor God in her relationships. This guide, "The Pursuit of Purity: A Christian Guide to Dating," seeks to provide a roadmap for individuals like Sarah who want to navigate the world of dating while remaining true to their Christian values.

In the chapters that follow, we will explore the principles of purity in dating, address the challenges that may arise, and offer practical advice for building God-honoring relationships. Together, we will delve into the art of communication, setting boundaries, understanding the role of family and friends, and seeking God's guidance in the process.

This journey is not just for Sarah but for all who seek to love and be loved in a way that aligns with their faith. Together, let us embark on this pursuit of purity, recognizing that, ultimately, our dating journey is a reflection of our love for God.

In the next chapter, we will dive into the importance of self-awareness and understanding our motivations as we begin our pursuit of purity in dating.

2

Self-Awareness and Motivation

Before you can embark on the journey of dating with purity, it's essential to understand yourself and your motivations. In this chapter, we will explore the critical elements of self-awareness and motivation, which lay the foundation for a God-honoring dating experience.

Know Thyself

The ancient Greek aphorism "Know thyself" is just as relevant today as it was in antiquity. Self-awareness is the cornerstone of healthy dating. It involves a deep understanding of your values, beliefs, and the desires of your heart. As a Christian, knowing your faith and what it means to you is paramount. It's about recognizing your strengths and weaknesses, understanding your past experiences, and embracing your unique identity as a child of God.

Motivations Matter

Why do you want to date? What drives your desire for a romantic relationship? Identifying your motivations is essential to ensure your dating journey is rooted in God's love. Common motivations include companionship, love, marriage, and the desire to start a family. While these are all valid and beautiful aspirations, it's important to ensure they align with your Christian values and your walk with God.

Guarding Your Heart

The Bible advises us in Proverbs 4:23 (NIV) to "above all else, guard your heart, for everything you do flows from it." This wisdom is particularly relevant to dating. To pursue purity in dating, you must safeguard your heart against impure motivations or ungodly desires. Guarding your heart means allowing God to guide your intentions and choices in the realm of dating.

Reflection and Prayer

Take time to reflect on your motivations for dating. In your prayer time, seek guidance from God. Ask Him to reveal any impure motivations and to help you align your heart with His will. Remember, God is your ultimate source of love and fulfillment. Your motivations should be a reflection of your desire to honor Him.

The Power of Accountability

In your quest for self-awareness and pure motivations, don't hesitate to seek accountability from trusted friends, family, or a mentor. Discussing your dating intentions and motivations with a fellow Christian can provide invaluable insights and help keep you on the path to purity.

Exercise: Motivation Journal

Consider keeping a motivation journal as you navigate your dating journey. In this journal, record your thoughts, feelings, and motivations regarding dating. Reflect on your progress and seek guidance from God through your writing. Over time, this journal can become a valuable tool for self-reflection and growth.

By understanding yourself and your motivations, you'll be better prepared to pursue purity in your dating life. In the next chapter, we will explore the importance of aligning your values with those of your potential partner, ensuring that your relationship is built on a strong, God-centered foundation.

3

Aligning Values in Christian Dating

As you continue your journey towards purity in dating, it's essential to recognize the significance of aligning your values with those of your potential partner. This chapter delves into the importance of shared beliefs, moral principles, and spiritual compatibility in building a strong, God-centered foundation for your relationship.

The Foundation of Shared Faith

One of the fundamental building blocks of a Christian dating relationship is a shared faith. The Apostle Paul asks in 2 Corinthians 6:14 (NIV), "Do not be yoked together with unbelievers. For what do righteousness and wickedness have in common? Or what fellowship can light have with darkness?" This verse emphasizes the importance of sharing a common faith with your partner, as it lays the groundwork for a relationship rooted in spiritual unity.

Deepening Spiritual Connection

To align your values, it's vital to foster a deep spiritual connection with your partner. Attend church services together, engage in shared Bible study, and pray together. These activities not only help you grow closer to God but also strengthen the bond between you and your partner.

Defining Your Shared Values

In addition to shared faith, take time to identify and discuss your shared values. What do you both hold dear in terms of ethics, family, community, and personal goals? Communicate openly about your beliefs and priorities to ensure you are on the same page when it comes to important life decisions and moral choices.

Communication is Key

Open and honest communication is the bedrock of aligning your values. Don't be afraid to have difficult conversations about your beliefs, boundaries, and expectations. It's through these dialogues that you can understand each other better and grow in your shared faith.

Balancing Individuality and Unity

While alignment in values is crucial, it's also essential to respect each other's individuality. Not every belief or value will be identical, and that's okay. What matters is that you both respect and support each other's unique journeys of faith while holding fast to your shared Christian beliefs.

Exercise: Values Discussion

Sit down with your partner and discuss your individual and shared values. Make a list of the beliefs and principles that are most important to you. Use this as a reference point throughout your dating journey to ensure that your values remain aligned.

The Path Forward

Aligning your values in Christian dating sets a strong foundation for your relationship. When your beliefs and principles are in harmony, you'll find it easier to navigate challenges, make important decisions, and grow together in faith. In the next chapter, we will explore the concept of setting healthy boundaries, which is crucial for maintaining purity in dating and honoring God in your relationship.

4

Setting Healthy Boundaries

In the pursuit of purity in Christian dating, setting healthy boundaries is an essential step. Boundaries are like fences that protect the garden of your relationship, ensuring that it grows in a healthy and God-honoring way. This chapter delves into the importance of setting boundaries and offers practical guidance on how to establish them.

Understanding Boundaries

Boundaries in dating are limits that define what is acceptable and unacceptable in your relationship. They help maintain emotional, physical, and spiritual purity. In 1 Corinthians 6:18 (NIV), we are reminded to "flee from sexual immorality." Setting boundaries is a practical way to follow this advice and remain pure in your relationship.

The Different Types of Boundaries

1. Physical Boundaries: These boundaries define the level of physical intimacy allowed in your relationship. It may include guidelines about kissing, holding hands, or more intimate physical contact.

2. Emotional Boundaries: Emotional boundaries protect your heart and mental well-being. They involve recognizing when to share deep feelings and when to hold back, as well as being honest about your emotional needs.

3. Spiritual Boundaries: Spiritual boundaries help maintain a focus on God in your relationship. This might involve setting aside time for prayer, attending church together, or discussing your spiritual journeys.

The Importance of Consent

Respecting each other's boundaries is vital. In a Christian dating relationship, both partners should willingly and enthusiastically agree on these limits. Consent is a fundamental principle in ensuring that the boundaries set are agreed upon by all parties involved.

Practical Tips for Setting Boundaries

1. Have a Conversation: Sit down with your partner and openly discuss your boundaries. Be honest about your needs and expectations, and encourage your partner to do the same.

2. Be Specific: Clarity is key. Define your boundaries as specifically as possible to avoid misunderstandings.

3. Be Flexible: While it's important to establish boundaries, be open to revising them as your relationship develops and both of you grow in your understanding of each other.

4. Involve Accountability: Share your boundaries with a trusted friend or mentor who can help keep you accountable and offer guidance.

Enforcing Boundaries

Setting boundaries is just the first step; enforcing them is equally important. This involves standing firm when the limits are tested and holding each other accountable. Remember that boundaries are not meant to be restrictive but rather liberating, allowing you to experience a relationship that is pure and God-centered.

Exercise: Boundary Agreement

Work with your partner to create a written agreement that outlines your agreed-upon boundaries. This document can serve as a reference point and reminder of your commitment to purity in your relationship.

The Path Forward

By setting healthy boundaries in your Christian dating relationship, you create a safe and pure space for your love to grow. Boundaries safeguard your emotional and spiritual well-being, allowing you to honor God in your journey. In the next chapter, we will explore the role of family and friends in supporting and guiding your relationship in the pursuit of purity.

5

The Role of Family and Friends in Your Christian Dating Journey

Family and friends play a significant role in your life, and their influence can be instrumental in your pursuit of purity in Christian dating. This chapter explores the importance of involving your loved ones in your relationship and offers guidance on how to maintain a balance between their input and your personal choices.

Godly Counsel

Proverbs 15:22 (NIV) says, "Plans fail for lack of counsel, but with many advisers, they succeed." Seeking the counsel of family and friends can provide valuable insights and guidance for your dating journey. Trusted individuals who share your Christian values can offer advice, perspective, and support that align with your faith.

Accountability Partners

Consider involving a close friend or mentor as an accountability partner in your relationship. This person can help you navigate challenges and ensure that you and your partner are upholding the standards and boundaries you've set. Accountability partners can pray with you, offer advice, and help you stay on course in your pursuit of purity.

Family Blessing

Incorporating family into your dating journey is a beautiful way to receive their blessings and support. When your family is involved, it can strengthen your relationship and add an extra layer of accountability. Additionally, having their support can bring peace and unity to your journey.

Setting Boundaries with Loved Ones

While involving family and friends in your dating journey is beneficial, it's essential to set boundaries with them as well. Make it clear to your loved ones what level of involvement and input you are comfortable with and where you need space for personal choices. Remember that your relationship is ultimately between you, your partner, and God.

Balancing Perspectives

While you should value the advice and input of your loved ones, remember that the final decision rests with you and your partner. God has given you free will, and as adults, you are responsible for making choices that align with your faith. Use the guidance of family and friends as a resource, but always approach decisions with prayer and discernment.

Exercise: Family and Friends Discussion

Engage in an open and honest discussion with your partner about how you both envision involving family and friends in your relationship. What roles and boundaries will you set? Understanding each other's perspectives and preferences will help you navigate this aspect of your journey.

The Path Forward

Including family and friends in your Christian dating journey can be a source of strength and support. Their guidance and blessings can help you stay on the path of purity while honoring God. In the next chapter, we will explore the significance of seeking God's guidance in your relationship and the role of prayer in your pursuit of purity.

6

Seeking God's Guidance Through Prayer

Prayer is the cornerstone of a Christian's relationship with God, and it is equally fundamental in the pursuit of purity in Christian dating. In this chapter, we delve into the significance of seeking God's guidance through prayer, both individually and as a couple, in your dating journey.

The Power of Prayer in Dating

Prayer is a direct line of communication with God, and it's essential to involve Him in every aspect of your relationship. In 1 Thessalonians 5:17 (NIV), we are encouraged to "pray continually." In your dating journey, prayer can help you maintain purity, make wise decisions, and deepen your connection with God.

Individual Prayer

Before embarking on a date or a significant step in your relationship, spend time in individual prayer. Seek God's guidance, ask for His wisdom, and pray for strength to maintain purity and stay aligned with His will. This individual prayer time allows you to center yourself and gain clarity on your intentions.

Praying as a Couple

Praying together as a couple is a powerful way to foster spiritual intimacy and ensure God remains at the center of your relationship. Praying for your partner and your relationship is an expression of your love and commitment. When praying as a couple, focus on the following aspects:

1. Thanksgiving: Express gratitude for your partner and the journey you're on together.

2. Guidance: Ask God for guidance in your relationship, seeking His wisdom in decisions and challenges.

3. Protection: Pray for protection against temptations and distractions that could lead you away from purity.

4. Strength: Request strength to uphold your boundaries and honor God in your relationship.

Listening to God

Prayer is not only about speaking but also about listening. As you pray individually and as a couple, create space for quiet moments, allowing God to speak to your hearts. Be open to His guidance, even if it doesn't align with your own desires or expectations. God's plan is always the best plan.

Prayer as a Source of Comfort

In moments of doubt or difficulty, prayer can provide comfort and peace. When you face challenges in your relationship, take them to God in prayer, seeking His guidance and solace. He is always there to provide support and understanding.

Exercise: Couple's Prayer Time

Set aside a specific time each day or week for prayer as a couple. Use this time to pray for your relationship, for each other, and for God's guidance. Be open and sincere in your prayers, sharing your desires and concerns with Him.

The Path Forward

Prayer is your direct connection to God, and it should be an integral part of your Christian dating journey. Seeking His guidance through prayer ensures that your relationship remains pure and God-centered. In the next chapter, we will explore the concept of patience in dating and the importance of trusting God's timing in your pursuit of purity.

7

Embracing Patience and Trusting God's Timing

In the pursuit of purity in Christian dating, patience and trust in God's timing are virtues that are often tested. This chapter delves into the importance of embracing patience and having faith that God's plan for your love life is perfect, even when it doesn't align with your expectations.

The Challenge of Patience

In a world where instant gratification is often the norm, patience can be a challenging virtue to uphold. In the context of Christian dating, patience means waiting on God's perfect timing for various aspects of your relationship, from its inception to its progression.

The Story of Ruth

The biblical story of Ruth beautifully illustrates the concept of patience and trusting in God's timing. Ruth's faith and patience led her to a loving and fulfilling relationship with Boaz. Her unwavering trust in God's plan for her life served as a testament to the power of patience and faith in Christian relationships.

Dating is a Journey, Not a Destination

Rather than viewing dating as a means to an end, consider it as a journey of personal growth and spiritual development. The pursuit of purity in dating is not solely about reaching a destination (marriage); it's about becoming the best version of yourself and growing closer to God along the way.

Trusting God's Timing

Proverbs 3:5-6 (NIV) advises us to "Trust in the Lord with all your heart and lean not on your understanding; in all your ways submit to him, and he will make your paths straight." Trusting God's timing means acknowledging that He knows what's best for you and your relationship. Sometimes, this may involve waiting for the right person or the right moment.

Letting Go of Control

One of the greatest challenges in embracing patience is letting go of the desire for control. Recognize that you cannot force a relationship to progress faster than God intends. Instead, surrender control and trust that God's plan is better than any plan you can devise.

Exercise: The Patience Journal

Keep a journal to document your thoughts and reflections on the concept of patience in your dating journey. Write about your struggles, your moments of trust, and how you're growing in patience. This journal can serve as a source of encouragement during difficult times.

The Path Forward

Embracing patience and trusting God's timing is an essential aspect of maintaining purity and honoring God in your dating journey. Remember that God's plan is perfect and that your patience will ultimately lead to a love story that is uniquely yours. In the final chapter, we will bring together all the elements of purity, faith, and love, summarizing the key principles of Christian dating.

8

A Recap of Christian Dating Principles

As we conclude this guide, it's time to reflect on the essential principles that have been explored throughout your journey in "The Pursuit of Purity: A Christian Guide to Dating." This chapter serves as a recap of the key principles that will guide you in your pursuit of purity in Christian dating.

1. Faith and Relationship Foundation

- Remember that a strong, shared faith is the foundation of a God-honoring Christian relationship.
   - Cultivate a deep spiritual connection with your partner through prayer, Bible study, and shared experiences of worship.

2. Self-Awareness and Motivation

- Start your dating journey by understanding yourself and your motivations.
   - Regularly evaluate your intentions and seek God's guidance to ensure your motivations remain pure and aligned with your faith.

3. Aligning Values

- Share your core values and beliefs with your partner.
  - Ensure that your values align to create a strong, God-centered foundation for your relationship.

4. Setting Healthy Boundaries

- Set clear and specific boundaries in the areas of physical, emotional, and spiritual intimacy.
  - Enforce these boundaries with love, respect, and accountability.

5. Involvement of Family and Friends

- Involve family and friends in your relationship to gain their support, blessings, and guidance.
  - Establish boundaries with your loved ones to maintain a balance between their input and your personal choices.

6. Seeking God's Guidance Through Prayer

- Prioritize prayer as a means of seeking God's guidance, individually and as a couple.
  - Embrace patience and trust in God's timing, and be open to listening to His guidance.

7. Embracing Patience and Trusting God's Timing

- Understand that Christian dating is a journey of personal and spiritual growth.
  - Trust in God's perfect timing and release the desire for control over your relationship.

As you apply these principles in your Christian dating journey, remember that the pursuit of purity is a continuous process. Your relationship with God should always be at the center of your love story. Upholding these principles will help you navigate challenges, make wise decisions, and ultimately create a relationship that reflects your faith and honors God.

Conclusion

"The Pursuit of Purity: A Christian Guide to Dating" is not merely a book; it's a guide for a lifetime of God-honoring relationships. Whether you are just starting your dating journey or seeking to renew your commitment to Christian principles in your current relationship, these principles will continue to be a source of guidance, strength, and inspiration.

In your pursuit of purity, never forget that God's love is the foundation of all love. His love, purity, and grace are the cornerstones of your faith, and they will guide you through the joys and challenges of your dating journey. May your pursuit of purity lead you to a love that is true, beautiful, and deeply rooted in Him.

9

Navigating Challenges and Preserving Purity

While Christian dating offers a beautiful path to love, it is not without its challenges. This final chapter will help you navigate common obstacles and preserve purity in your relationship, ensuring that your commitment to God remains unwavering.

1. Temptations and Maintaining Boundaries

In the course of your relationship, you may encounter temptations that challenge the boundaries you've set. It's essential to remain vigilant and rely on prayer, accountability, and open communication to overcome these challenges. Remember, God provides strength in moments of weakness.

2. Conflict Resolution

Conflicts are a natural part of any relationship. How you handle them can have a significant impact on your pursuit of purity. Practice conflict resolution with love, humility, and a focus on finding solutions that align with your faith and values.

3. External Pressures

External pressures from societal norms, media, or even well-meaning friends and family can create tension in your relationship. Stay committed to your Christian values and make decisions that honor God, even if they diverge from what the world suggests.

4. Uneven Spiritual Growth

You and your partner may experience uneven spiritual growth. Be patient and supportive, understanding that each person's faith journey is unique. Encourage each other to grow spiritually, seek God's guidance, and pray for a deepening of your faith as a couple.

5. Trusting in God's Plan

Through all the challenges and uncertainties, trust in God's plan for your relationship. Even when your path doesn't seem clear, know that God is guiding you. Continually seek His wisdom and trust in His divine timing.

Exercise: Purity Renewal

Take time with your partner to renew your commitment to purity in your relationship. Revisit your boundaries and pray together, asking for God's strength to preserve them. This exercise can serve as a reminder of your dedication to purity.

Conclusion: The Eternal Pursuit

"The Pursuit of Purity: A Christian Guide to Dating" has guided you through the principles and practices that will help you maintain a pure and God-honoring dating journey. While challenges may arise, remember that your pursuit of purity is an eternal one. It's not just for your dating phase; it's a commitment you carry with you into every stage of your relationship, including marriage.

As you continue to pursue purity in your relationship, let it be a testament to your love for God and your dedication to His plan. With faith, prayer, and unwavering commitment to your Christian values, you can create a love story that reflects His grace, mercy, and everlasting love.

May your journey be filled with the blessings of a love that is pure, steadfast, and deeply rooted in your faith.

10

Celebrating Your Love Story

As you near the conclusion of this guide, it's time to celebrate your love story. This final chapter is a reminder that the pursuit of purity in Christian dating is not just about overcoming challenges; it's about rejoicing in the beautiful, God-honoring love you've nurtured. In this chapter, we'll explore how to celebrate your love story and continue growing in your faith as a couple.

Reflect on Your Journey

Take a moment to reflect on your dating journey. Remember the moments when you first met, the hurdles you overcame, the growth you've experienced together, and the love that has blossomed. Celebrate the unique path that brought you to this point.

Share Your Testimony

Your love story is a testimony of your faith and your commitment to pursuing purity in dating. Share your experiences with others, both as a source of inspiration and as a testament to God's presence in your relationship. Your story may encourage others in their pursuit of purity.

Plan Moments of Gratitude

Create intentional moments of gratitude and celebration in your relationship. This could involve:

- Celebrating your dating anniversary with a special meal, outing, or prayer of thanksgiving.
    - Marking milestones in your faith journey, such as baptisms, church events, or mission trips.
    - Recognizing the growth in your relationship through periodic reflections and expressions of gratitude.

Continue Growing Spiritually

A Christian relationship is a lifelong journey of spiritual growth. Dedicate yourselves to deepening your faith together. Attend church services, engage in Bible study, and commit to prayer as a couple. Strive to grow in your faith individually and as a partnership.

Exercise: Love Letter to Each Other

Write love letters to each other, celebrating your relationship, your shared faith, and the joy of pursuing purity in your love story. Share these letters in a special moment of connection.

Conclusion: The Beginning of Forever

Your pursuit of purity in Christian dating is just the beginning of a love story that can last a lifetime. As you continue to celebrate and grow in your love, remember that God is the center of your relationship. With His guidance, your love story can be a beacon of hope, purity, and enduring commitment.

Celebrate your love story, and let it be a testament to God's love and grace. May your relationship continue to reflect His light, mercy, and everlasting love as you move forward into the future, hand in hand.

11

Nurturing a Lasting, God-Honoring Relationship

As your journey through "The Pursuit of Purity: A Christian Guide to Dating" continues, this chapter focuses on nurturing a lasting and God-honoring relationship. Beyond the dating phase, building a strong and enduring relationship founded on purity and faith is an ongoing endeavor.

1. A Lifelong Commitment

Christian dating doesn't end when you enter into a romantic relationship or get married. It's a commitment that extends throughout your entire life together. Continue to prioritize purity, faith, and a deep connection with God in every phase of your relationship.

2. Ongoing Communication

Communication remains a cornerstone of a healthy relationship. Continue to communicate openly, honestly, and lovingly with your partner. As your relationship grows, discuss your dreams, fears, and goals to ensure you're always on the same page.

3. Encourage Each Other's Faith

Support each other's spiritual journeys and growth. Encourage regular Bible study, prayer, and engagement in church or spiritual activities. Share your spiritual insights and be a source of strength in moments of doubt.

4. Practice Forgiveness and Grace

Inevitably, challenges and conflicts will arise. Practice forgiveness, extending grace to your partner as God extends grace to us. This fosters a spirit of reconciliation and understanding.

5. Grow as a Team

See your relationship as a partnership in which you both grow and evolve. Set goals, plan for the future, and work together to achieve your dreams. Recognize that your love story is a shared journey.

Exercise: Goal-Setting Together

Sit down with your partner and set both short-term and long-term goals for your relationship. These could include spiritual growth goals, personal milestones, or dreams you wish to achieve together. Goal-setting helps you stay aligned and motivated.

Conclusion: A Love Story Woven with Faith

Nurturing a lasting, God-honoring relationship is a journey that continues for a lifetime. As you remain committed to purity, faith, and love, your relationship will be a testimony to the enduring power of God's grace and the beauty of a love story deeply rooted in faith.

Remember that God is at the center of your relationship, and His love is the guiding force that will lead you through all seasons of your life together. Your pursuit of purity is an eternal commitment, and as you continue on this path, may your love story shine as a beacon of His love and grace.

12

Passing on the Legacy of Purity

As we conclude this guide, it's essential to reflect on the importance of passing on the legacy of purity to future generations. Your commitment to God-honoring dating and relationships can have a profound impact on those who come after you. This chapter explores how you can impart this legacy to others.

1. Leading by Example

The most powerful way to pass on the legacy of purity is by living it. Your love story, founded on Christian values, serves as an example to family, friends, and those who observe your relationship. Demonstrating purity in your dating journey will inspire others to follow suit.

2. Mentorship and Discipleship

Consider becoming mentors or spiritual guides to individuals who are beginning their own dating journeys. Sharing your experiences, wisdom, and the lessons you've learned can provide valuable guidance to those who seek to navigate Christian dating with purity.

3. Family and Parenting

For those who enter into the next phase of family life, parenting is an opportunity to instill the principles of purity in your children. Teach them the importance of faith, purity, and God-centered relationships. Create a loving and faith-based environment where they can grow and develop their own understanding of purity.

4. Supporting and Encouraging Others

Support and encourage others in their pursuit of purity. This can include actively participating in church groups or community programs that promote God-honoring relationships. Share resources and knowledge, and be a source of encouragement for those seeking purity in their relationships.

5. Advocacy and Outreach

Consider getting involved in advocacy and outreach efforts that promote purity and faith-based dating. By contributing your time, talents, and knowledge, you can help spread the message of purity to a wider audience and inspire others to pursue God-honoring relationships.

Exercise: Legacy Building

Reflect on the ways you can pass on the legacy of purity in your own life. Set specific goals for how you'll contribute to this legacy, whether through mentorship, parenting, advocacy, or community involvement. Create an action plan to put your ideas into practice.

Conclusion: The Everlasting Impact

Your commitment to the pursuit of purity in Christian dating can have a lasting and profound impact on generations to come. By living and sharing the principles of faith, purity, and love, you contribute to a legacy that reflects God's grace and mercy.

May your love story be a testament to the enduring power of God's love and serve as a guiding light for others seeking the path of purity in their own relationships. Your legacy is a gift to the world, one that reflects the beauty of God-honoring love.

Book Summary: The Pursuit of Purity: A Christian Guide to Dating

"The Pursuit of Purity: A Christian Guide to Dating" is a comprehensive and insightful guide that provides a roadmap for individuals seeking to build God-honoring relationships. In this guide, readers are taken on a journey through the principles and practices that underpin Christian dating, with a primary focus on maintaining purity, faith, and a deep connection with God throughout the dating process.

The book is structured into twelve chapters, each addressing key aspects of Christian dating. It begins with the foundational importance of faith in a Christian relationship. From understanding the significance of shared faith to deepening the spiritual connection with a partner, the book emphasizes that faith is the cornerstone upon which a God-honoring relationship is built.

Self-awareness and motivation take center stage in Chapter 2, highlighting the importance of knowing oneself and the motivations driving the pursuit of dating. Through reflection, prayer, and seeking accountability from trusted individuals, readers are encouraged to align their intentions with their Christian values.

Chapter 3 delves into aligning values, emphasizing the critical role shared beliefs and principles play in creating a strong, God-centered foundation for a relationship. The importance of open communication, especially regarding values, is highlighted.

In Chapter 4, the book explores the establishment and enforcement of healthy boundaries in a dating relationship. This chapter underscores the significance of boundaries in maintaining emotional, physical, and spiritual purity, along with practical tips for setting and enforcing them.

Chapter 5 delves into the role of family and friends in supporting and guiding a Christian dating relationship. It suggests involving loved ones while setting clear boundaries to maintain a balance between their input and personal choices.

The pivotal role of prayer is examined in Chapter 6, where readers are encouraged to seek God's guidance through individual and couples' prayer. The chapter also emphasizes the importance of embracing patience and trusting God's timing in one's dating journey.

In Chapter 7, readers are urged to navigate challenges and preserve purity in their relationship. Topics include addressing temptations, conflict resolution, external pressures, and uneven spiritual growth.

Chapter 8 summarizes the key principles discussed throughout the book, reminding readers of the importance of faith, values, boundaries, and trust in God's plan.

The subsequent chapter, Chapter 9, focuses on nurturing a lasting and God-honoring relationship, underlining the importance of ongoing communication, support for each other's faith journey, and practicing forgiveness and grace.

In Chapter 10, the guide encourages readers to celebrate their love story by reflecting on their journey, sharing their testimony, and planning moments of gratitude and spiritual growth.

The final chapter, Chapter 11, highlights the significance of passing on the legacy of purity to future generations, emphasizing leading by example, mentorship, family and parenting, supporting and encouraging others, and advocacy and outreach efforts.

"The Pursuit of Purity: A Christian Guide to Dating" is a comprehensive and thoughtful guide that not only provides practical advice for navigating the complexities of dating as a Christian but also reinforces the importance of maintaining purity, faith, and a deep connection with God in the pursuit of a God-honoring relationship. This guide is a valuable resource for individuals seeking to embrace a faith-based approach to dating and relationship-building, ensuring that their love stories reflect the beauty of God's grace and everlasting love.

www.ingramcontent.com/pod-product-compliance
Lightning Source LLC
LaVergne TN
LVHW020456080526
838202LV00057B/5985